Best-Ever
Activities for Grades 2–3

Graphing

**Dozens of Activities With Engaging Reproducibles That
Kids Will Love . . . From Creative Teachers Across the Country**

BY JACQUELINE CLARKE

SCHOLASTIC
PROFESSIONAL BOOKS

New York • Toronto • London • Auckland • Sydney • Mexico City
New Delhi • Hong Kong • Buenos Aires

For Garrett, who fills our house and minds
with number talk each and every day!

Many thanks to the teachers who contributed ideas to this book:
Marianne Chang, Kelley Foster, Pamela Galus, Trina Licavoli Gunzel, Dan Kriesberg,
Judy Meagher, Ruth Melendez, Deborah Rovin-Murphy, Charlotte Sassman,
Wendy Weiner, and Elizabeth Wray.

"Birthdays" from ALL TOGETHER NOW by Sonja Dunn.
Copyright ©1999 by Pembrook Publishers. Reprinted by permission of Pembrook Publishers.

Produced by **Joan Novelli**
Cover and interior design by **Holly Grundon**
Cover and interior art by **Paige Billin-Frye**

ISBN 0-439-29645-5

CONTENTS

CONTENTS

About This Book

Kids are born collectors! At a very young age, they acquire great numbers of rocks, trading cards, action figures, fast-food meal toys, and a vast array of other objects. They repeatedly sort, count, and re-count their collections and love to watch the numbers grow as they add new pieces.

In school, we can build on these first experiences with graphing to help students make sense of the information-rich society in which they live, and to help them become informed citizens and intelligent consumers. We know they will be easily drawn into the process of collecting data, but we must be equally sure that they know how to organize and present the information they gather. According to the National Council of Teachers of Mathematics (NCTM) *Principles and Standards 2000,* students need to learn to "formulate questions that can be addressed withdata… collect, organize, and display relevant data to answer them…develop and evaluate inferences and predictions that are based on data."

This book is filled with activities that teach students how to collect, organize, and describe data. The activities are drawn from all areas of the curriculum and provide opportunities for students to work individually, in small groups, and as a class. As you flip through the book, you'll see activities to teach line, bar, circle, and picture graphs, as well as other ways to organize data—for example, by using glyphs, coordinate grids, and Venn diagrams. Here's what else you'll find:

- ideas from teachers around the United States

- activities that correlate with the NCTM standards

- lots of reproducible activity pages, including poetry, games, graphic organizers, and more

- literature and poetry links

- multiple intelligences links, with suggestions for integrating art, writing, movement, and music with graphing

- strategies for second-language learners

- test-taking tips

- assessment tips

- suggestions for interactive morning messages

- take-home activities to involve families in student learning

- and many more activities that involve kids in active graphing!

Story Time Graph

Help students see how they can use graphs to make shared decisions, such as what book to read during story time.

Choose two books and display them on the chalkboard ledge. Invite students to preview them during snack time or recess. Give each child a clothespin. Ask children to vote for the book they would like read during story time by clipping the clothespin to the cover. When everyone has had a chance to vote, gather children around the books and ask the following questions:

- What do the clothespins represent?
- How many students wanted to read _____ for story time? (Repeat with the other title.)
- How many more students wanted to read _____ than _____?
- Which book will we be reading today? Why?

TiP

Use graphs to involve students in other classroom decisions such as what topics to study, where to go for field trips, or when to have recess.

Art

Photo Faces

Be prepared for your next graphing experience with these reusable, student-created graph markers.

Take a head shot of each child (or have children bring in photos from home). Give each child half an index card. Have students glue their photos to the center of the card, and create a decorative border around the edges. Laminate the index card graph markers for durability. When it's time to graph, have students attach their personalized markers to the surface using Velcro®, masking tape, or removeable wall adhesive. A quick glance at the remaining markers will tell you which students have missed their turn!

Kelley Foster
Cicero Elementary School
Cicero, New York

Let's Talk Graphing Word Wall

Encourage your students to "talk math" by creating a word wall of graphing terms.

- Ask students to name words that relate to the topic of graphing. List each word on a separate index card.

- Arrange the words in a brick formation on a bulletin board. Label the board, "Math Is Spoken Here!"

- As you continue to study graphing, add new "bricks" to the wall.

- Use the wall to play word games such as Pictionary. Let students take turns choosing a word and drawing it on the chalkboard for classmates to guess. The first child to name the word correctly takes the next turn.

Marianne Chang
Schilling School
Newark, California

SECOND Language LEARNERS

Work with second-language learners to create their own picture dictionary of graphing terms. On each page of a student-made book, record one of the words from the wall. Invite children to illustrate their books to provide picture clues for math vocabulary.

Look What I'm Reading!

Are your students reading from different genres? Use graphs to track their preferences.

Make one copy of the bar graph for each student. (See page 34.) Review the different genres listed on the horizontal axis. Share a sample book for each and invite children to add titles they've read that fit in the various categories. (Poetry, Informational, Science Fiction/Fantasy, Mystery, Biography, Folklore, Realistic Fiction, Historical Fiction)

Instruct students to record the titles of books they read in the appropriate columns on their own graphs. Meet with students on a regular basis to review their graphs. In which genres are they reading the most books? the fewest? Use this information to encourage them to explore other genres.

Add these graphs to students' language arts portfolios. Let children use them at open school night or conferences to show their families what types of books they're reading.

Graph a Story

Use a line graph to plot the intensity of main events and show students how stories develop.

Work together with children to record the main events of a story in chronological order on a sheet of chart paper. Assign each event a number and record these numbers on the horizontal axis of a line graph. Label the axis "Story Events." Number the vertical axis from 1-10 and label it "Intensity Scale." Rate each event on the line graph using the intensity scale. Ask students to look at the graph and find the climax of the story. Discuss the position of the climax in relation to other events. Explain that authors often use this pattern to tell a story. Invite students to use line graphs to plot the events of other books they are reading.

Graphing Freewrite

"Freewriting" is a timed exercise in which students record their thoughts continuously about a specific subject without regard for grammar or spelling. Here's how you can apply this technique to reading and interpreting graphs.

Use the overhead projector to display a graph from the newspaper or an old textbook. Set a timer for five minutes and invite students to write as much as they can about the graph—for example, "This is a bar graph. It has two columns. It surveyed 88 children. It shows that 42 children prefer creamy peanut butter and 46 prefer crunchy. Four more children prefer crunchy to creamy." When the timer rings, ask children to share what they've written. Record the cumulative responses on a sheet of chart paper. Discuss and categorize the different types of information gathered. Use this chart as a resource the next time you ask children to talk or write about a graph.

Repeat this technique using a different type of graph. Use students' responses to assess how well they are able to read and understand graphs.

SECOND Language LEARNERS

To allow second-language learners to focus more fully on the graphing freewrite activity, allow them to dictate their responses as you write them. At the end of the five minutes, read what you have written to the student. Have the child then read it back to you. This process reinforces writing, reading, and oral language skills in a meaningful context.

Weekly Spelling Words Graph

Use this graphing activity to reinforce weekly spelling (or vocabulary) words—and build writing skills.

- Write spelling (or vocabulary) words on index cards. Place them in a pocket chart.

- Invite students to examine the words and think of a way to graph them. For example, words may be graphed according to their part of speech, number of syllables, or spelling pattern. Once the category is determined, use index cards to label the columns of the graph in the pocket chart. Hand out words to students and let them take turns sorting the words into the correct columns on the graph. Repeat the activity using different categories.

Graphing Journal

As you study graphing, use journals to move students from talking about graphs to writing about them.

To create the journals, have children cut sheets of graph paper in half and place a dozen or so sheets together, then staple to bind. Have students create a cover for their graph journals, writing their name on it and illustrating with graphing words or pictures of graphs. Throughout the year, students can use their journals to:

- explain the results of a graph
- define graphing terms
- keep track of data
- compare data within a graph
- create different types of graphs using the same information
- record equations that tell about a graph
- compute the mean, median, and mode

TIP

Let children share their journals with families at conference time or open-school night to illustrate what they've been learning about graphing.

Good Morning Lil' Gridders

Use your morning message as a vehicle for discussing and interpreting graphs.

In the morning message, ask students to graph their response to a question that affects the entire class—for example, "What should we study next: amphibians or reptiles?" Include a graph for children to mark responses on in the morning message. Add cloze sentences to get students thinking about the graph—for example:

- ⑥ _____ students want to study amphibians.
- ⑥ _____ students want to study reptiles.
- ⑥ We will be studying _____!

When everyone has had a chance to graph their response, let volunteers fill in the blanks using the results of the graph. Encourage students to write additional cloze sentences about the graph for others to complete.

SECOND Language LEARNERS

It's always a good idea to give students practice with graphing in a real-life context, such as graphing votes for the next science topic, or the next read-aloud. However, be aware that for second-language learners the words may get in the way of the math. To help with this situation, look at graphs for specific vocabulary that may not be familiar to second-language learners—for example, in the above activity, the words *amphibian* and *reptile* may be unfamiliar. Make sure you've identified and defined this vocabulary ahead of time. This procedure does double duty. Not only does it ensure that second-language learners will get to participate in the graphing activities and share what they know, it will also help them increase their English vocabulary. Support second-language learners as they fill in the blanks of the cloze sentences by making number lines available to assist with interpreting the graph.

Story Stacks

Graph students' library books to determine whether they are selecting more fiction or nonfiction.

As students return from the library, ask them to sort their books into two piles, one labeled "Fiction" and the other "Nonfiction." Gather children around the stacks of books. Ask: "Which stack is higher? Does this mean that more fiction or nonfiction was chosen? How can we tell for sure?" Work together with students to count the books in each pile. Create stacks of interlocking cubes to represent each type of book. Ask: "Did you choose more fiction or nonfiction books at the library today? How many more? How many books did the class borrow altogether?" Repeat this activity for several weeks and compare the results. Do students consistently choose one type of book over the other? Ask students to explain their preferences.

FICTION   NON-FICTION

Take-Home Activity:
Four-Seasons Pictograph

Connect math, science, and language arts with a graph that invites students to survey friends and family members to find out which season they like best.

Give each student a copy of the poem "Four Seasons." (See page 35.) Read the poem aloud. Discuss the words the poet used to describe each season. Have children take the poem home and share it with friends and family. Instruct them to use the pictograph at the bottom of the page to survey and color in one icon for each person's favorite season. When students return to school with their graphs, ask them to write a paragraph telling why they think one season was favored over another. Encourage them to include their personal thoughts on the season they like best.

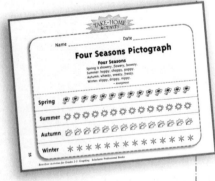

Ready, Set, Graph!

Set up a graphing center in your classroom to set the stage for easy and creative graphing experiences.

On a table or low shelf, place graphing materials such as index cards, markers and tape in small baskets or plastic containers. Include a variety of items to use as graphing markers—for example, sticky notes, clothespins, laminated name tags, photo faces (see page 6), interlocking cubes, magnets, or milk caps (from half-gallon or gallon jugs). Provide slips of paper on which students may record their own ideas for graphing questions. Make a pad of chart paper available (or a white board) and invite children to create survey graphs that their classmates can respond to. Use the wall space above the materials to display completed graphs as well as newspaper clippings showing other graphs, charts, tables, or interesting data.

Judy Meagher
Student Teacher Supervisor
Bozeman, Montana

Graph of the Week

When students are involved in the process, adding graphing to your weekly routine is a snap!

At the beginning of the school year, ask each student to think of and record one graphing question on a sentence strip. Questions might include "What color are your eyes? How many people are in your family?" Each week choose one student's question and challenge him or her to design and/or assemble the weekly graph. Let the same student lead the class in a discussion of the graph by asking questions about the data gathered—for example, "How many more students _____ than _____?" This student might also guide the class in calculating the mode and range.

Marianne Chang
Schilling School
Newark, California

Set aside one bulletin board in your classroom or hallway to display your weekly graphs.

Substitute Teacher Graph

Students are surprised when they find their teacher absent. Help ease the transition by having this graphing activity waiting for your substitute to use.

Label a three-column bar graph with the following categories: Home Sick, At a Meeting, and Out of Town. Label the graph "Where Do You Think Your Teacher Is Today?" Copy a class set of a picture of yourself for students to use as graph markers. (You could also have children draw a picture of you on index cards cut in half.) On the day of your absence, instruct the substitute to have students graph their predictions of your whereabouts. Provide questions for discussing the graph, such as: "How many students think their teacher is home sick? How many more students think their teacher is at a meeting out of town?" Be sure to let the substitute know the reason for your absence so he or she can share this with students.

Literature LINK

Miss Nelson Is Missing

by Harry Allard (Houghton Mifflin, 1985)

If you're going to be absent, don't forget to leave the substitute a copy of this book. While students ponder your whereabouts, they can hear the story of the kids in Room 207, who long for Miss Nelson's return when they find themselves in the hands of the new substitute, Miss Viola Swamp.

Three-Way Graph

Show students how the same information can look different by varying the intervals on a graph.

Write test scores for an imaginary student on the chalkboard—for example, 88, 92, 94, 90, and 92. Ask students to plot the scores on three different graphs using the following intervals:

- by tens from 0 to 100
- by fives from 85 to 120
- by ones from 87 to 95

Invite students to look at the graphs they've created. Ask: "Which graph would you rather show your parents? Which graph looks like your test scores are very poor? Which graph looks like you study a lot sometimes and not at other times?"

Dan Kriesberg
Locust Valley Intermediate School
Locust Valley, New York

Work with students to create graphs for their own test scores. Share the graphs with parents at conference time.

Tracking-Time Table

Help students evaluate how they use their time by tracking the number of minutes spent on various activities.

For five days have students use the table on page 36 to track the time they spend on six different activities. They need to make one tally mark for every five minutes. At the end of the week, ask them to record the total number of minutes for each activity in the space provided. Using the data they gather, have them prepare a graph to illustrate how they used their time. Invite students to write a reflective paragraph explaining what they have learned from their tracking-time table and graph. How will this experience affect how they use their time in the future?

Ruth Melendez
High Plains Elementary School
Colorado Springs, Colorado

Collection Graph

Create a graph to help both students and teachers keep track of permission slips or other forms that must be returned to school.

- Collect enough frozen-juice can lids to equal the number of students. Rinse and dry the lids thoroughly.

- Have students glue their photos to the underside of a lid. Attach a piece of magnetic tape to the reverse side.

- Write Yes and No at the bottom of a magnetic chalkboard. Line up all the graph markers in the No column. Place a collection box near the graph. As students return their forms, have them move their marker to the Yes column.

- At the end of each day, ask students to check the graph. Use the data to guide a quick discussion that doubles as a reminder. Ask: "How many students have brought in their permission slips? How many more need to bring them in?" Make reminder notes available for students still in the No column.

TIP

To create reusable game boards, glue grids to file folders and laminate. Students can use removable wall adhesive to position treasure chests, and wipe-off markers to record hits and misses.

Treasure Hunt!

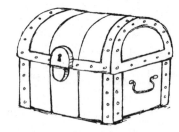

Use this version of the classic game Battleship™ to help students locate points on a coordinate grid.

- To make a game board, tape two coordinate grids (see page 37) to the inside of a file folder (one on each side). Each player will need one game board. Make copies of the treasure chests on page 38, and give one to each player.

- Divide the class into pairs and instruct partners to sit facing one another. Place an object, such as a plastic storage tub, between them (to block each player's view of the other's game board). Have children position their game boards so that the bottom half lies flat on the desk while the top half is propped up against the object in between the two players.

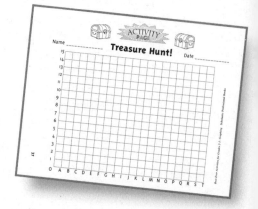

- To begin the game have players position a treasure chest so that it covers 15 squares on the top half of the game board, vertically or horizontally. Players can tape or glue their treasure chests in place or make reuseable game boards. (See Tip, page 16.)

- Players then take turns calling out points on the grid in an attempt to locate their opponent's treasure. "Hits" and "Misses" are recorded in red and green crayon, respectively, on the bottom half of the game board. The winner is the first player to locate all 16 points that surround their opponent's treasure.

Button Graph

Move students through a series of graphs to help them understand the concepts of concrete, representational, and symbolic. You'll need to have a button for each child to complete the activity.

- Use index cards to label columns of a floor graph from 0 to 10. Ask students to stand in the column that shows how many buttons are on the clothes they are wearing. Explain that this is a real graph because we are using real people (ourselves), instead of objects to represent us.

- Have students step off the graph and place a photo marker (see Photo Faces, page 6) in the spot where they stood. Define this graph as representational because the pictures look like and stand for us.

- Finally, ask students to replace their photo marker with a button. Explain that this graph is called symbolic because the button is a symbol for us, but it in no way looks like us.

- On a sheet of posterboard, create a permanent, symbolic graph using the buttons. Discuss the graph and challenge students to calculate the total number of buttons worn by the entire class.

To make a floor graph, purchase a shower curtain from a discount store. Create a grid on the curtain using strips of masking tape. As students participate in other graphing experiences, ask them to identify the type of graph as concrete, representational, or symbolic.

Class-Photo Graph

Show students how to use a Venn diagram to organize information about themselves and others.

blue eyes   wears glasses

⑤ To prepare for the activity, record students' physical characteristics on index cards—for example, blue eyes, curly hair, or wears glasses. Glue student photos to small squares of cardboard or clean frozen-juice can lids. Draw a Venn diagram on a sheet of posterboard and laminate.

⑤ Choose two index cards, such as brown eyes and curly hair. Tape them beneath the two circles. Work together with students to sort the photo markers into the different categories. A student who has both brown eyes and curly hair will place his or her photo in the space where the two circles intersect. A student who has neither brown eyes nor curly hair will place his or her photo in the space outside the two circles.

⑤ Display the Venn diagram and ask, "How many students have brown eyes? How many students have curly hair? How many students have both brown eyes and curly hair? How many students have neither brown eyes nor curly hair? In which category are the most students? the least?" Repeat the activity several times using different physical characteristics.

TIP

Check for food allergies before letting children eat their cereal graph markers.

Cereal Snack Graph

With this colorful graph, students learn how to write equations to represent data.

Give each child a small bag of multi-colored O-shaped cereal pieces and a sheet of large-square graph paper. Show students how to sort their cereal by color, as shown. Based on the total number of cereal pieces in each column, have them write equations for:

⑤ blue + red (repeat using other color combinations)

⑤ the three primary colors (red + blue + yellow)

⑤ the two colors that make green (blue + yellow)

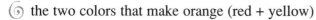

- the two colors that make orange (red + yellow)
- the two colors that make purple (red + blue)
- the colors of grass and sky (green + blue)
- the three colors of a traffic light (red + yellow + green)
- their two favorite colors

Invite students to transform their real graphs into symbolic ones. Have them remove (and eat) their cereal pieces one at a time and color in the squares to replace each one accordingly.

**Kelley Foster
Cicero Elementary School
Cicero, New York**

Change the color equations to reflect the cereal you use.

Take-Home Activity:
Graphing Goes Home

Help parents reinforce what their children are learning in school with a take-home letter that lists fun ways to explore graphing at home.

Give each child a copy of the take-home letter on page 39. Read through the checklist together to review ways they can learn about graphing at home. Ask children to check off the activities as they try them. They can set a personal goal for the number of activities, or you may recommend a number. As students return the checklists to school, encourage them to bring in samples of the work they completed to share with classmates. Display their at-home graphing projects on a bulletin board with a sign that reads Graphing Goes Home!

Pick Your Pop!

Create a graph using two-liter bottles to determine which type of soda students like best.

- ⑤ Collect six empty 2-liter bottles. Label each with a different flavor of soda: root beer, cola, orange, grape, lemon-lime, and cherry.

- ⑤ Set the bottles on a table and ask, "Which type of soda would you pick?"

- ⑤ Let students cast their vote by pouring a half-cup of water into the bottle that represents their favorite. Use a funnel to avoid spills.

- ⑤ Draw students' attention to the height of water in each bottle. Let students tell you which type of soda is the most popular and which is the least popular.

- ⑤ Ask: "How can we determine the number of students that voted for each type of soda?" To do this, pour the contents of each bottle into a large, glass measuring cup. Double the number of cups to determine the number of students.

Take-Home Activity:
Graphing by the Slice

Based on a survey of favorite pizza toppings, students create circle graphs to display the results.

- ⑤ Send each child home with a copy of the pizza slices and toppings. (See page 40.) Instruct students to survey six friends and/or family members to find out which pizza topping they like best: plain cheese, pepperoni, mushroom, sausage, or veggie. For each response, have them cut out the topping and glue it to a slice. For plain cheese responses, slices should be left as is.

- ⑤ Once students have all six responses, have them cut out the slices, sort them by topping, and glue them in a circle formation to another sheet of paper. They can use extra copies of the toppings to create a key for the graph.

- ⑤ Back at school, help children record fractional amounts and/or percentages to show how many people preferred each topping. Display the circle graphs on a bulletin board with a sign that reads "Graphing by the Slice."

TIP

You may want to add food coloring to the water to make the graph easier to read.

Coordinate Twister

In this adaptation of a favorite floor game, students use their hands and feet to plot coordinates on a giant grid.

⑤ Use strips of masking tape to create a grid on the classroom floor that has 20 squares and is approximately 4 by 5 feet. Use index cards to label the horizontal axis with letters (A, B, C, D, E) and the vertical axis with numbers (1, 2, 3, 4).

⑤ Use index cards to make a set of body part cards that include right foot, left foot, right hand, and left hand. Use a different color of index cards to make coordinate cards in all of the possible combinations: A, 1; A, 2; A, 3; A, 4; B, 1; B, 2; B, 3; etc.

⑤ Shuffle both sets of cards. Choose two players and one caller. Have the caller stand with his or her back to the grid and select a body part and coordinate card to give each player a movement command. For example, a player might have to place her left foot on E, 4. When a player is unable to follow a command or remain upright, he or she is replaced by another player and a new round begins.

Literature LINK

The Fly on the Ceiling

by Dr. Julie Glass (Random House, 1998)

Introduce students to coordinate grids with this humorous math myth. This book tells the story of French philosopher René Descartes and how he discovered the Cartesian Coordinate system while looking for a way to organize all his "stuff"!

When test time rolls around, let students flip through their graphing journals (see page 10) to review and explain what they've learned about graphing.

Data Detectives

Challenge students to search through books, newspapers, magazines, and the Internet for interesting information suitable for graphing.

- Show students examples of data you've discovered in the media—for example, daily temperatures from cities across the country or sports scores. Work together to create graphs from this data to serve as models for students' own work.

- Have students search for data at home, using any of the resources mentioned. (You might also make copies of the daily paper available for students to borrow.) Ask students to clip or copy the information (being sure to record the data source), and bring it to school.

- Help students decide which type of graph (line, bar, circle, etc.) would best represent the information they've found. Supply markers and posterboard and invite them to create graphs based on their data. Remind students of the models they created earlier and encourage them to use them as resources.

- Provide time for students to share their graphs with classmates. As they do, ask them to identify the data source and to explain why they chose a particular type of graph.

Literature LINK

The Factastic Book of 1001 Lists
by Russell Ash (Dorling Kindersley, 1999)

This fact- and figure-packed book is a great source of graphing data. Look for information on everything from animals to the arts. Kids can graph the ocean depth, high (and low) temperatures, wingspan, sound levels, building height, sports scores, and the measurement of each planet.

TIP

Students can use programs such as *Data Wonder* (Addison Wesley), *TableTop Jr.* (TERC), and *The Graph Club* (Tom Snyder) to create graphs on the computer.

TIP

USA Today is a great source of colorful graphs, charts, and tables.

Graphing in the News

In this activity, students make real-world connections as they read and interpret graphs in the newspaper.

Invite students to scan the newspaper for several days until they find a graph that interests them. Have them glue the graph on a sheet of paper and write the answers to the following questions:

- What is the title of this graph?
- What does this graph tell you? Name three things.
- Who might benefit from this information?
- What type of graph is used to represent the data?
- What is the source of this information?

Display the graphs on a bulletin board and let students compare and contrast them.

As an alternative activity, have students write five questions about their graph beside it on their paper. Let students exchange papers and answer one another's questions.

Take-Home Activity:
Coordinate Maps

For an activity that is sure to hit home, invite kids to use coordinate grids to create a map of their bedroom. To first model this assignment, work together with students to create a coordinate map of the classroom or playground.

- Send each student home with a copy of the coordinate grid. (See page 41.)

- Challenge students to create a map of their bedroom by plotting only those objects that take up floor space such as a bed, dresser, bookshelf, chair, or toy box. Have them write the name and/or draw a picture of the object next to each point.

- On a separate sheet of paper, ask students to write five questions based on their map—for example, "Where is my bed? What object can be found at point (6, 5)?" Invite students to exchange papers and answer one another's questions.

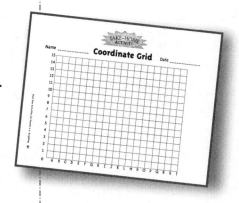

Monday's Child

Inspired by a traditional rhyme, students investigate and graph the day of the week on which they were born.

⊚ Share the poem "Monday's Child" with students. (See page 42.) Have them find out the day of the week they were born on and fill in the last line of the poem.

⊚ Make seven extra copies of the cake pattern and label them with the days of the week. Glue the cakes to a large sheet of craft paper. Give each child a birthday candle. Have children glue their candles to the cake that shows their birthday. Gather children around the graph. Count the number of students born on each day. Ask questions such as:

> On which day of the week were the most (and fewest) students born?

> How many more students were born on Monday than Tuesday?

⊚ Reread the poem, then ask: "Which line tells about you?" Invite students to tell whether they think their line accurately depicts them. Make new poems by letting children rewrite the line of the poem so it accurately reflects their personality and interests—for example, "Monday's child is good at sports."

Bottles and Cans Pictograph

Let students create a pictograph to show the number of bottles (plastic) and cans they collect during a school-wide charity drive.

⊚ Plan a recycling drive to raise money for a charity of your students' choice. Have students work together to create flyers and posters to advertise the event. Place a large garbage can in an accessible location to house the donations.

TIP

Students may be able to find out on which day of the week they were born by asking their parents. They can also find this information on the Internet at **highhopes.com/ 21centurycalen dar.html**.

- Collect for five days. Near the end of each day, bring the bottles and cans back to the classroom. Work with students to tally the total number of each. Provide students with gloves to handle the donations. (The school nurse may be able to provide disposable gloves for this.)

- When the week is over, help students create a pictograph to show how many bottles and cans were collected each day. Make multiple copies of the bottle and can templates on page 43. Have students color them and cut them out. To make the graphs (one for bottles, one for cans), label the horizontal axis with the days of the week that correspond to the drive. For each day, have students cut and paste one bottle or can for every two collected. If the total number is odd, show students how to cut a bottle or can in half to represent one bottle.

- Post the completed graphs and ask questions to guide a discussion: "On Monday, did we collect more cans or bottles?" (repeat for other days of the week) "On which day did we collect the most cans? bottles? both? How many cans did we collect altogether? bottles? both? How much money is each bottle/can worth? How much money will the bottles raise for charity? cans? both?"

- Extend the activity by creating a line graph to show how much money is collected from the drive each day. Display the graphs in the school lobby with a big sign saying "Thank You!" Take the cans/bottles to a recycling center and donate the proceeds to charity.

And the Survey Says . . .

Invite students to create and conduct surveys to learn more about fellow classmates.

- Copy your class list on a survey form and make a copy for each student. Ask each student to come up with a survey question and two to five suitable responses—for example, "How much sleep do you get on a weeknight: 8 hours or less, more than 8 hours but less than 9 hours, from 9 to 10 hours, more than 10 hours."

- Have students work over a period of a few days to gather responses from each of their classmates, then summarize the data in a graph. Put their graphs together to make an informative class book!

Trina Licavoli Gunzel
Lincoln Elementary School
Corvallis, Oregon

TIP

You may want to begin with a concrete graph using the real bottles and cans. Then, for every two bottles/cans you remove from the concrete graph, glue one bottle/can to the pictograph.

Take-Home Activity:
Graphing Goes to Work!

How are graphs used in the workplace? Challenge students to find out!

- Ask students to survey parents, grandparents, and friends of the family to discover how they use graphs, charts, or tables in their work. Encourage them to bring in at least one example to share with the class.

- As students share their examples, encourage them to identify the line of work and explain how the graph, chart, or table is used.

- Use these workplace models to create a bulletin board display. Randomly scatter sheets of graph paper over colorful bulletin board paper to create a backdrop for the examples. Label the display "Graphing Goes to Work!"

Before-and-After Graph

Planning an insect unit? As an introductory activity, use a scatter graph to assess children's attitudes about insects.

- To create the graph, make two copies of the ladybug pattern on page 44. Write Yes at the bottom of one and No on the other. Tape the ladybugs to the chalkboard under the question, "Do You Like Insects?"

- Give each student a black sticky dot. Ask students to graph their response to the question by placing their dot on the corresponding ladybug. Together, count up each ladybug's spots to determine how many students do or do not like insects.

- Readminister the graph after your insect unit and compare the results. Have attitudes changed? Ask students to reflect on why or why not their thoughts about insects might be different.

Wendy Weiner
The Parkview School
Milwaukee, Wisconsin

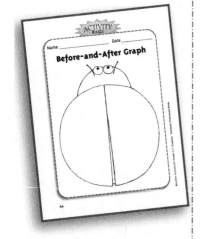

Try other before-and-after graphs with students as you study bats, spiders, or snakes!

Shape Scatter Graphs

Let students learn more about scatter graphs with an activity that lets them survey parents at open-school night or parent conferences.

- Ask each student to think of a graphing question with no more than three responses—for example, "What kind of ice cream do you like: chocolate, strawberry, or vanilla?"

- Show them how to create a shape graph by drawing and cutting out a large shape or shapes that correspond to their question—for example, an ice cream cone with three different scoops for the above question.

- Ask students to write the question on a sentence strip and hang it along with their scatter graph at a display. During open-school night or at conferences, give parents a sheet of sticky dots. Invite them to use the dots to respond to each graph.

- The next day, ask students to write a few sentences telling about the data they've collected on their shape graph.

Judy Meagher
Student Teacher Supervisor
Bozeman, Montana

TIP

Guide students in making several scatter graphs to respond to as a class before assigning them to create their own.

SECOND Language LEARNERS

You may want to have second-language learners dictate their survey questions for you to record. After writing them on the form, let the students read back the questions. This will strengthen word recognition skills in meaningful ways and help children participate more fully in the activity. If any of your second-language learners need assistance reading classmates' names, give them a blank survey form and have them ask students to record their name when asked the survey question. They can read the name back to themselves, reinforcing spelling and pronunciation.

Garden Graph

Use a line graph to compare the growth of two plants, and spark spin-off explorations on seeds and plants.

- Purchase two different bulbs (for example, amaryllis and narcissus) from a garden store. Let students plant them in pots and place them in a suitable spot (indoors) for growing.

- Label the horizontal axis of a line graph with the number of weeks (10) and the vertical axis with the number of inches (20). Each week measure and record the height of each plant using the line graph.

- Use two differently colored markers to distinguish between the two plants. Once both bulbs are fully-grown, discuss the graph:

    How many weeks did it take for the amaryllis bulb to bloom? the narcissus bulb?

    How many inches did the amaryllis grow altogether? the narcissus?

    Which bulb grew the fastest? the tallest?

    Looking at the data for the amaryllis [narcissus] bulb, which week showed the most growth? the least growth?

Charlotte Sassman
Alice Carlson Applied Learning Center
Forth Worth, Texas

Take the activity further by letting children work in teams to design a similar experiment to track and graph growth of other plants.

Graph a Snack

Show students how to use a graph to compare the fat content of their favorite snacks. Use what students learn to guide lessons on nutrition.

- Collect mini-size (1 oz.) empty commercial snack bags that students bring in their lunch, such as those for potato chips, pretzels, or cheese twists. Once you have duplicate bags for four or five different kinds of snacks, create a line graph by gluing one set of the bags (one of each type) to the horizontal axis of a graph. Label the vertical axis from 0 to 15 to represent the number of fat grams per bag.

- Pass out the extra bags you've collected and show students how to read the nutritional information on the package. Explain that *g* is an abbreviation for grams and help them locate the number of fat grams in each bag. Provide nutritional information to help students discover how much fat they need in their diets each day.

- Record the fat grams for each type of snack on the graph. Ask: "How many grams of fat do the pretzels have?" (Repeat for each type of snack.) "Which snack contains the highest amount of fat? least? How does the amount of fat in your favorite snack compare with the amount of fat you need each day? Which snack is the healthiest? Why?"

Elizabeth Wray
Blair Middle School
Norfolk, Virginia

Grow-a-Beast Graph

Use attention-getting "grow beasts" for an investigation that lets students create line graphs to record and compare the data they collect.

- Purchase two identical grow beasts at a craft or discount store. Show them to students and ask them to predict whether the beasts will grow larger in salt water or distilled water.

- Place the beasts in separate containers of the same size. Fill each container with a different type of water (distilled or salt) and place them in the same area of the room to control for light, airflow, and surrounding temperature.

- At the same time each day, remove the beasts from the containers. Drop them from a height of one foot to knock off excess moisture. Use a balance scale to obtain the mass in grams of each beast. Set up a table to record the data.

- Repeat the process for 12 days. At the end of this period, ask each child to create a line graph showing time versus mass for each beast. Use the graphs to discuss the results of the experiment. Ask children why they think the distilled-water beast grew larger than the salt-water beast. (The answer is related to the concept of *diffusion*—when particles from two or more substances intermingle. In the plain water, there are fewer particles inside the "beast" than outside so the water is free to move into the creature, making it larger. In the salt water, there are more particles outside the beast. The water will move into the beast until there is an equal amount outside and inside.)

Pamela Galus
Burke School
Omaha, Nebraska

Encourage students to create similar graphs based on other nutritional data such as calorie or carbohydrate counts. For nutritional information, including the recommended daily allowances for fat and other nutrients, go to **www.usda.gov**.

Dinosaur Data

Given a set of clues, students uncover and graph the height of five dinosaurs.

⟲ Give each student a copy of the Dinosaur Data sheet. (See page 45.) Ask children to read each clue at the top of the page. Show them how to use the information to calculate and graph each dinosaur's height.

⟲ Encourage students to look at the completed graph and make other comparisons among the dinosaurs—for example, how many spikes, length of tails, and so on. Students can make visual representations of the comparisons for a fun display.

For more dinosaur fun take your students to kidsdomain.com /games/dino. html, where they can play a coordinate game called "Dinosaur Dig."

Literature LINK

How Big Were the Dinosaurs?

by Bernard Most (Harcourt Brace, 1994)

This book invites children to make comparisons between the size of dinosaurs and everyday objects, such as a school bus. For more comparisons, see *The Littlest Dinosaurs* (Harcourt Brace, 1989), also by Bernard Most.

Graphing Animal Data

Science is full of interesting facts and figures! During your next animal unit invite students to create graphs using amazing animal data.

⟲ Divide the class into six groups. Give each group a different animal data card. (See page 46.) Challenge children in each group to

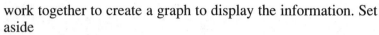

work together to create a graph to display the information. Set aside
time for each group to share their graph.

ⓖ Encourage them to ask each other questions—for example, "Why did you choose to display your data on a bar graph? What was the greatest challenge for you in creating this graph?" Display the graphs in the hallway for other classes to enjoy.

Weather Watchers

Help your young meteorologists track and graph the weather using the local newspaper.

ⓖ Make copies of the newspaper weather page for each student. Draw students' attention to the various types of data shown, such as temperature highs and lows, rain and snowfall amounts, wind speeds, and times of sunrise and sunset.

ⓖ Each month choose one type of data to collect. As part of your morning routine, record the previous day's data on your calendar grid, using the newspaper as a resource. At the end of the month, help students decide on the best type of graph to display the information collected. Let pairs of children lead the class in creating the graph each month. Place graphs in a binder to create an almanac so that students can easily revisit the graphs and build on their understandings.

Musical Pictograph

After listening to musical selections, students graph the type of music they enjoy most.

ⓖ Choose five musical selections, one each from the following categories: jazz, classical, country, rock and roll, and new age. Ask students to listen attentively as you play each song.

ⓖ Replay a small portion of each song and invite students to stand up when they hear the type of music that best represents their preference. Create a table on the chalkboard to record the number of students for each musical category. Work together with students to create a pictograph of their musical preferences.

Instead of giving each group a different animal data card, give each group a copy of the same card. Challenge children to create different types of graphs from the same information.

How Long Are Their Tails?

Asian Elephant
59 inches

Leopard
55 inches

African Elephant
51 inches

African Buffalo
43 inches

Giraffe
43 inches

Red Kangaroo
43 inches

Not Your Average Tail!

In this activity, students calculate the mean, median, mode, and range of six lengthy animal tails.

- Divide the class into six groups. Assign each group a different animal. (See How Long Are Their Tails?, left.) Using various art materials and the measurements given, instruct each group to create the animal's tail and record the length on it.

- Display the tails vertically on a wall or bulletin board. Make sure they are even at the top. Challenge students to determine the range, mean, median, and mode of the tails.

Take-Home Activity:
Hidden-Picture Graph Packs

With this take-home activity, students plot and connect points to reveal a hidden picture.

- Make one copy of the coordinate cards (see page 47) and cut them apart. Place each one in a resealable, plastic bag along with crayons and a copy of the coordinate grid. (See page 41.)

- Show students how to use the cards to plot and connect the points in order on the grid. Encourage them to personalize their pictures by adding color and details.

- Make the picture packs available for students to sign out on a daily or weekly basis. Invite students to create their own picture packs to share with classmates. To do so, they should first draw a design on the grid and then list the coordinate pairs on an index card.

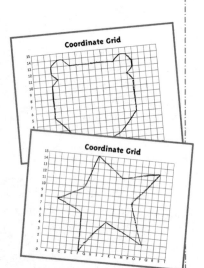

Deborah Rovin-Murphy
Richboro Elementary School
Richboro, Pennsylvania

Graphs on the Move

With this physical graph, students use movement to respond to the question "During which month were you born?"

- Read aloud "Birthdays." (See page 48.) As you do, invite students to reveal their birth month by responding with the movements named in the chant. For example, children born in September will touch their toes.

- Read aloud the chant a second time, this time having a volunteer "data collector" tally the number of students for each month. (Be sure this child counts him- or herself, too.) Create a bar graph to display the data collected.

- Fill in the squares in each column using crayons in colors that match each month's birthstone. (See Birthstone Colors, below.)

Birthstone Colors

Month	Stone	Color
January	Garnet	Red
February	Amethyst	Purple
March	Aquamarine	Light Blue
April	Diamond	Clear or Yellow
May	Emerald	Green
June	Pearl	White
July	Ruby	Red
August	Peridot	Light Green
September	Sapphire	Blue
October	Opal	White
November	Topaz	Yellow
December	Turquoise	Blue

Name _____

Date _____

Look What I'm Reading!

Historical Fiction					
Realistic Fiction					
Folklore					
Biography					
Mystery					
Sci Fi/ Fantasy					
Informational					
Poetry					

Name _____

Date _____

Four Seasons Pictograph

Four Seasons

Spring is showery, flowery, bowery.
Summer: hoppy, choppy, poppy.
Autumn: wheezy, sneezy, freezy.
Winter: slippy, drippy, nippy.

— *Anonymous*

Spring

Summer

Autumn

Winter

Best-Ever Activities for Grades 2-3: Graphing Scholastic Professional Books

Name _____

Date _____

Tracking-Time Table

Activity	Amount of Time					Weekly Total
	Monday	Tuesday	Wednesday	Thursday	Friday	
Doing Homework						
Watching TV						
Playing Sports						
Playing						
Doing Chores						
Using a Computer						

Best-Ever Activities for Grades 2-3: Graphing Scholastic Professional Books

36

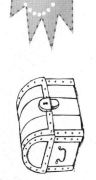

ACTIVITY PAGE

Treasure Hunt!

Name _____

Date _____

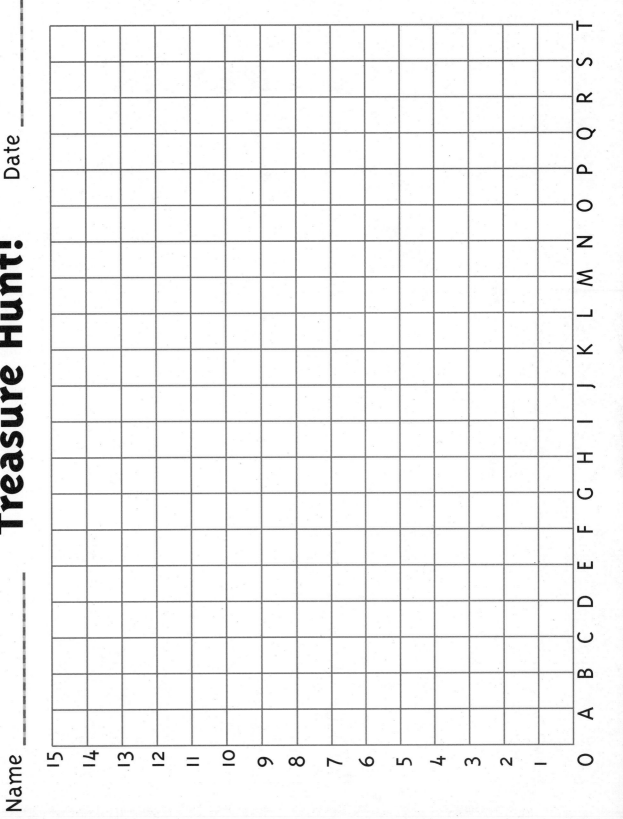

15
14
13
12
11
10
9
8
7
6
5
4
3
2
1
O   A B C D E F G H I J K L M N O P Q R S T

Name _____ Date _____

Treasure Hunt!

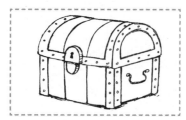 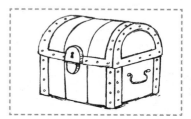

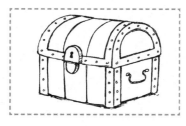 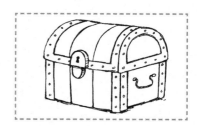

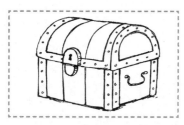 

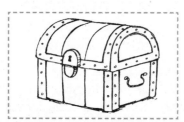 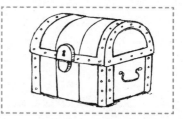

Best-Ever Activities for Grades 2-3: Graphing Scholastic Professional Books

Name _____ Date _____

Graphing Goes Home

Dear Families,

The world is full of data! Every day televisions, radios, computers, newspapers, and magazines are filled with weather statistics, sports scores, consumer reports, and trivia. To prepare for life in this information-rich society, your child is learning how to collect, display, and use data through a variety of graphing experiences. Here are some quick-and-easy activities you can do with your child to build graphing skills at home. Please check off any activities you try together and return this letter to school by _____.

☐ Bring home graphs, charts, or tables that you use at work and share them with your child. Discuss how these tools help you in your job.

☐ If your child watches or participates in sports, let him or her create a graph or table to keep track of related data.

☐ Ask your pediatrician for a copy of your child's growth chart. During which years did he or she grow the most? the least?

☐ As you read the newspaper, clip graphs, charts, or tables to share with your child. Keep them in a scrapbook and let your child create trivia questions based on the data to amuse friends and family.

☐ Use a table to keep track of household chores and/or responsibilities your child completes. After several weeks, examine the data and discuss the results. Are there certain jobs that always get done while others are often neglected?

☐ Ask your child to draw a raindrop on the calendar for each day that it rains. At the end of the month, help him or her create a graph to show how many days it rained each week.

Name _____   Date _____

Graphing by the Slice

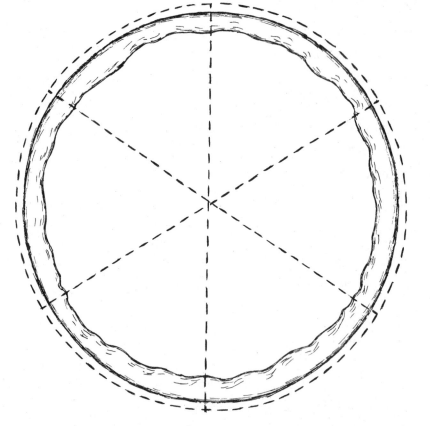

pepperoni

mushroom

sausage

veggie

Best-Ever Activities for Grades 2–3: Graphing Scholastic Professional Books

Name _____

Coordinate Grid   Date _____

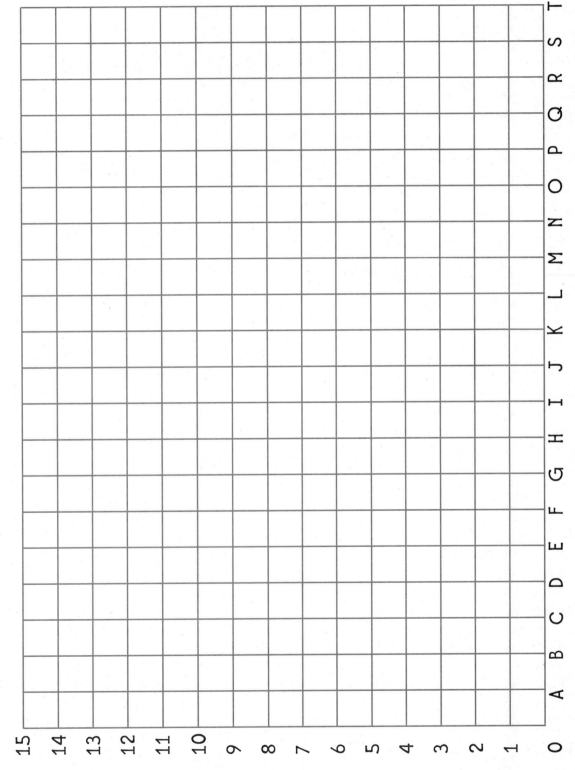

Name _____   Date _____

Monday's Child

Monday's child is fair of face,
Tuesday's child is full of grace,
Wednesday's child is nice to know,
Thursday's child is on the go,
Friday's child is loving and giving,
Saturday's child makes life worth living,
And the child who is born on the seventh day,
Makes many friends along the way!
I was born on a _____!

—adapted by Jacqueline Clarke

Color candles on the cake to show how old you are.
Write in the name for the day of the week on which you were born.

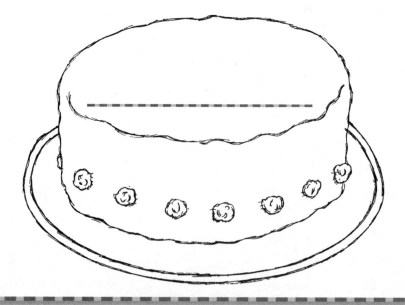

Best-Ever Activities for Grades 2-3: Graphing   Scholastic Professional Books

Name _____   Date _____

Bottles and Cans
Pictograph

Best-Ever Activities for Grades 2-3: Graphing   Scholastic Professional Books

Name _____ Date _____

Before-and-After Graph

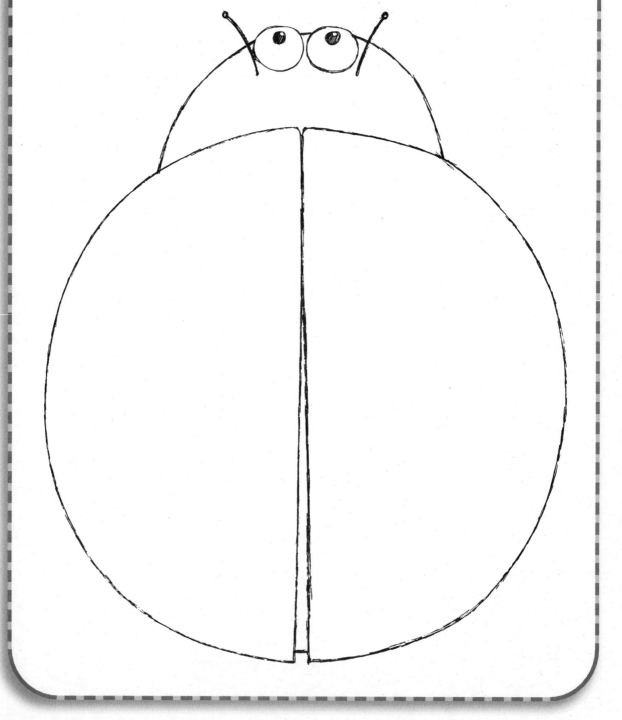

Best-Ever Activities for Grades 2-3: Graphing Scholastic Professional Books

Name _____ Date _____

Dinosaur Data

Clues

1. Tyrannosaurus Rex was 50 feet tall.

2. Ultrasaurus was twice as tall as Tyrannosaurus Rex.

3. Diplodocus was 10 feet shorter than Ultrasaurus.

4. It would take three Stegosauruses to equal the height of Diplodocus.

5. Stegosaurus and Triceratops were the same height.

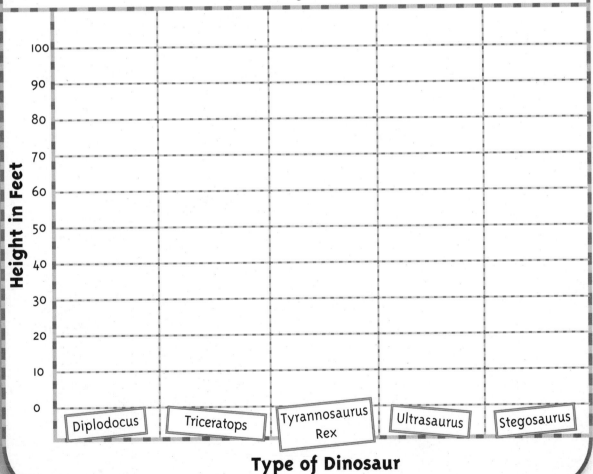

Height in Feet

100
90
80
70
60
50
40
30
20
10
0

Diplodocus   Triceratops   Tyrannosaurus Rex   Ultrasaurus   Stegosaurus

Type of Dinosaur

Name _____ Date _____

Graphing Animal Data

How Long Can They Stay Underwater?

Mammal	Number of Minutes
Human	1
Sea Otter	5
Platypus	10
Hippopotamus	15
Seal	22

How Long Do They Sleep?

Animal	Average Hours of Sleep per Day
Koala	22
Tow-Toed Sloth	20
Little Brown Bat	19
Giant Armadillo	18
Child	10

How Fast Does Their Heart Beat?

Animal	Heartbeats Per Minute
Bat	750
Cat	120
Sheep	75
Horse	40
Frog	30

How Fast Can They Swim?

Animal	Miles Per Hour
Sailfish	68
Bluefin Tuna	46
Yellowfin Tuna	44
Blue Shark	43
Wahoo	41

How Long Can They Live?

Animal	Years
Giant Tortoise	150
Human	121
Killer Whale	90
Common Toad	40
Queen Ant	18

How Much Do They Weigh?

Mammal	Weight in Tons
Blue Whale	128
Fin Whale	44
Gray Whale	32
Humpback Whale	26
Pilot Whale	3

Name _____ Date _____

Hidden-Picture
Graph Packs

1. (H,15)	8. (L,8)
2. (G,14)	9. (N,10)
3. (F,14)	10. (N,12)
4. (D,12)	11. (L,14)
5. (D,10)	12. (K,14)
6. (F,8)	13. (J,15)
7. (I,0)	

1. (F,13)	11. (K,1)
2. (E,14)	12. (M,2)
3. (D,14)	13. (P,5)
4. (C,13)	14. (P,10)
5. (C,12)	15. (O,11)
6. (D,11)	16. (P,12)
7. (C,10)	17. (P,13)
8. (C,5)	18. (O,14)
9. (F,2)	19. (N,14)
10. (H,1)	20. (M,13)

1. (G,14)	10. (M,1)
2. (C,12)	11. (P,6)
3. (A,9)	12. (S,4)
4. (A,6)	13. (R,7)
5. (B,6)	14. (R,8)
6. (B,5)	15. (S,11)
7. (A,5)	16. (P,9)
8. (C,2)	17. (N,12)
9. (E,1)	18. (J,14)

1. (H,15)	6. (J,5)
2. (F,10)	7. (P,2)
3. (A,8)	8. (N,8)
4. (F,6)	9. (R,13)
5. (F,0)	10. (L,12)

Best-Ever Activities for Grades 2-3: Graphing   Scholastic Professional Books

Name _____   Date _____

Birthdays

Hey, hey
When's your birthday?

Clap your hands
If it's January

Stamp your feet
If it's February

Shrug your shoulders
If it's March

If it's April
Up you stand

Born in May
Wave your hand

June's the month
To touch the sky

Fly around
If it's July

If it's August
Blow your nose

In September
Touch those toes

If your day is in October
Start that day
By rolling over

In November
Bend your knees

Here's December
You must freeze!

— *Sonja Dunn*

"Birthdays" from ALL TOGETHER NOW by Sonja Dunn. Copyright ©1999 by Pembrook Publishers. Reprinted by permission of Pembrook Publishers.
Best-Ever Activities for Grades 2-3: Graphing Scholastic Professional Books

48